I0224778

THE GREAT OPERAS OF

Giacomo Puccini

—

An Account of the Life and Work of this Distinguished
Composer, with Particular Attention to his Operas.

Illustrated with Portraits in Costume and Scenes from Opera.

—

By
GUSTAV KOBBÉ

—

Copyright © 2018 Read Books Ltd.
This book is copyright and may not be
reproduced or copied in any way without
the express permission of the publisher in writing

British Library Cataloguing-in-Publication Data
A catalogue record for this book is available from
the British Library

A History of The Theatre

'The Theatre' is a collaborative form of fine art that uses live performers to present the experience of a real or imagined event. The performers may communicate this experience to the audience through combinations of gesture, speech, song, music, and dance, with elements of art, stagecraft and set design used to enhance the physicality, presence and immediacy of the experience. The specific place of the performance is also named by the word 'theatre' – derived from the Ancient Greek word *théatron*, meaning 'a place for viewing', itself from *theáomai*, meaning 'to see', 'watch' or 'observe'.

Modern Western theatre largely derives from ancient Greek drama, from which it borrows technical terminology, classification into genres, and many of its themes, stock characters, and plot elements. The city-state of Athens is where 'theatre' as we know it originated, as part of a broader culture of theatricality and performance in classical Greece that included festivals, religious rituals, politics, law, athletics, music, poetry, weddings, funerals, and symposia. Participation in the city-state's many festivals – and attendance at the City Dionysia as an audience member (or even as a participant in the theatrical productions) in particular, was an important part of citizenship.

The theatre of ancient Greece consisted of three types of drama: tragedy, comedy, and the satyr play (a form of tragicomedy, similar in spirit to the bawdy satire of burlesque). The origins of theatre in ancient Greece, according to Aristotle (384–322 BCE), the first theoretician of theatre, are to be found in the festivals that honoured Dionysus. These performances (the aforementioned City Dionysia) were held in semi-circular auditoria cut into hillsides, capable of seating 10,000–20,000 people. The stage consisted of a dancing floor (orchestra), dressing room and scene-building area (skene). Since the words were the most important part, good acoustics and clear delivery were paramount. The actors (always men) wore masks appropriate to the characters they represented, and each might play several parts.

Athenian tragedy (the oldest surviving form of tragedy) emerged sometime during the sixth century BCE, and flowered during the fifth century BCE – from the end of which it began to spread throughout the Greek world – and continued in popularity until the beginning of the Hellenistic period. Aeschylus, Sophocles, and Euripides were masters of the genre. The other side of the coin – Athenian comedy, is conventionally divided into three periods; 'Old Comedy', 'Middle Comedy', and 'New Comedy'. Old Comedy survives today largely in the form of the eleven surviving plays of Aristophanes, while Middle Comedy is largely lost (preserved only in a few relatively short fragments in authors such as Athenaeus of Naucratis). New Comedy is known primarily from the substantial papyrus fragments of Menander.

Western theatre developed and expanded considerably under the Romans. The theatre of ancient Rome was a thriving and diverse art form, ranging from festival performances of street theatre, nude dancing, and acrobatics, to the staging of Plautus's broadly appealing situation comedies, to the high-style, verbally elaborate tragedies of Seneca. Although Rome had a native tradition of performance, the Hellenization of Roman culture in the third century BCE had a profound and energizing effect on Roman theatre and encouraged the development of Latin literature of the highest quality for the stage. This tradition fed into the modern theatre we know today, and during the renaissance, theatre generally moved away from the poetic drama of the Greeks, and towards a more naturalistic prose style of dialogue. By the nineteenth century and the Industrial Revolution, this trend continued to progress.

In England, theatre was immensely popular, but took a big pause during 1642 and 1660 because of Cromwell's Interregnum. Prior to this, 'English renaissance theatre' was witnessed, with celebrated playwrights such as William Shakespeare, Christopher Marlowe and Ben Jonson. Under Queen Elizabeth, drama was a unified expression as far as social class was concerned, and the Court watched the same plays the commoners saw in the public playhouses. With the development of the private theatres, drama became more oriented towards the tastes and values of an upper-class audience however. By the later part of the reign of Charles I, few new plays were being written for the public theatres, which sustained themselves on the accumulated works of the previous decades. Theatre was now seen as something sinful and the Puritans tried very hard to drive it out of their society. Due to this stagnant period, once Charles II came back to the throne in 1660, theatre (among other arts) exploded with influences from France, and the wider continent.

The eighteenth century saw the widespread introduction of women to the stage – a development previously unthinkable. These women were looked at as celebrities (also a newer concept, thanks to ideas on individualism that were beginning to be born in Renaissance Humanism) but on the other hand, it was still very new and revolutionary. Comedies were full of the young and very much in vogue, with the storyline following their love lives: commonly a young roguish hero professing his love to the chaste and free minded heroine near the end of the play, much like Sheridan's *The School for Scandal*. Many of the comedies were fashioned after the French tradition, mainly Molière (the great comedic playwright), again harking back to the French influence of the King and his court after their exile.

After this point, there was an explosion of theatrical styles. Throughout the nineteenth century, the popular theatrical forms of Romanticism, melodrama, Victorian burlesque and the well-made plays of Scribe and Sardou gave way to the problem plays of Naturalism and Realism; the farces of Feydeau; Wagner's operatic *Gesamtkunstwerk*; musical theatre (including Gilbert and Sullivan's operas); F. C. Burnand's, W. S. Gilbert's and Wilde's drawing-room comedies; Symbolism; proto-Expressionism in the late works of August Strindberg and Henrik Ibsen; and Edwardian musical comedy. The list continues! These trends continued through the twentieth century in the realism of Stanislavski and Lee Strasberg, the political theatre of Erwin Piscator and Bertolt Brecht, the so-called Theatre of the Absurd of Samuel Beckett and Eugène Ionesco, and the rise of American and British musicals.

Theatre itself has an incredibly long history, and despite the massive proliferation of theatrical styles and mediums – it essentially owes its existence to the ancient Greeks and the Romans. The three main genres; tragedy, comedy and satyre, continue to influence plot themes, directing, writing and acting, with frequent and fascinating interrelations and overlaps. As a genre, it remains as popular today as it has ever been, and continues as a massive influence on popular culture more broadly. It is hoped that the current reader enjoys this book on the subject.

Giacomo Puccini

(1858–   )

THIS composer, born in Lucca, Italy, June 22, 1858,
first studied music in his native place as a private
pupil of Angeloni. Later, at the Royal Conservatory,
Milan, he came under the instruction of Ponchielli, composer of "La Gioconda," whose influence upon modern
Italian opera, both as a preceptor and a composer, is regarded as greater than that of any other musician.

Puccini himself is considered the most important figure
in the operatic world of Italy today, the successor of Verdi,
if there is any. For while Mascagni and Leoncavallo each
has one sensationally successful short opera to his credit,
neither has shown himself capable of the sustained effort
required to create a score vital enough to maintain the
interest of an audience throughout three or four acts, a
criticism I consider applicable even to Mascagni's "Lodo-
letta," notwithstanding its production and repetitions at
the Metropolitan Opera House, New York, which I believe
largely due to unusual conditions produced by the European
war. Puccini, on the other hand, is represented in the repertoire of the modern opera house by four large works:
"Manon Lescaut" (1870), "La Bohème" (1896), "Tosca"
(1900), and "Madama Butterfly" (1904). His early two-
act opera, "Lea Villi" (The Wilis, Dal Verme Theatre, Milan,
1884), and his three-act opera, "La Fanciulla del West"
(The Girl of the Golden West), 1910, have been much less

Giacomo Puccini

successful; his "Edgar" (La Scala, Milan, 1889), is not heard outside of Italy. And his opera, "La Rondine," has not at this writing been produced here, and probably will not be until after the war, the full score being the property of a publishing house in Vienna, which, because of the war, has not been able to send copies of it to the people in several countries to whom the performing rights had been sold.

LE VILLI

"Le Villi" (The Wilis), signifying the ghosts of maidens deserted by their lovers, is the title of a two-act opera by Puccini, words by Ferdinando Fortuna, produced May 31, 1884, Dal Verme Theatre, Milan, after it had been rejected in a prize competition at the Milan Conservatory, but revised by the composer with the aid of Boïto. It is Puccini's first work for the lyric stage. When produced at the Dal Verme Theatre, it was in one act, the composer later extending it to two, in which form it was brought out at the Reggio Theatre, Turin, December 26, 1884; Metropolitan Opera House, N. Y., December 17, 1908, with Alda (*Anna*), Bonci (*Robert*), Amato (*Wulf*).

Of the principal characters *Wulf* is a mountaineer of the Black Forest; *Anna*, his daughter; *Robert*, her lover. After the betrothal feast, *Robert*, obliged to depart upon a journey, swears to *Anna* that he will be faithful to her. In the second act, however, we find him indulging in wild orgies in Mayence and squandering money on an evil woman. In the second part of this act he returns to the Black Forest a broken-down man. The Wilis dance about him. From *Wulf's* hut he hears funeral music. *Anna's* ghost now is one of the wild dancers. While he appeals to her, they whirl about him. He falls dead. The chorus sings "Hosanna" in derision of his belated plea for forgiveness.

The Complete Opera Book

Most expressive in the score is the wild dance of the Wilis, who "have a character of their own, entirely distinct from that of other operatic spectres" (Streatfield). The prelude to the second act, "L'Abbandono," also is effective. Attractive in the first act are the betrothal scene, a prayer, and a waltz. "Le Villi," however, has not been a success outside of Italy

"Manon Lescaut," on the other hand, has met with success elsewhere. Between it and "Le Villi" Puccini produced another opera, "Edgar," Milan, La Scala, 1889, but unknown outside of the composer's native country.

MANON LESCAUT

Opera in four acts, by Puccini. Produced at Turin, February 1, 1893. Covent Garden, London, May 14, 1894. Grand Opera House, Philadelphia, in English, August 29, 1894; Wallack's Theatre, New York, May 27, 1898, by the Milan Royal Italian Opera Company of La Scala; Metropolitan Opera House, New York, January 18, 1907, with Caruso, Cavalieri, and Scotti. The libretto, founded on Abbé Prévost's novel, is by Puccini, assisted by a committee of friends. The composer himself directed the production at the Metropolitan Opera House.

CHARACTERS

MANON LESCAUT...*Soprano*
LESCAUT, sergeant of the King's Guards..................*Baritone*
CHEVALIER DES GRIEUX ....*Tenor*
GERONTE DE RAVOIR, Treasurer-General...................*Bass*
EDMUND, a student.....................................*Tenor*
Time—Second half of eighteenth century.
     Place—Amiens, Paris, Havre, Louisiana.

Act I. plays in front of an inn at Amiens. *Edmund* has a solo with chorus for students and girls. *Lescaut, Geronte,* and *Manon* arrive in a diligence. *Lescaut* is taking his sister to a convent to complete her education, but finding her to be greatly admired by the wealthy *Geronte*, is quite willing to play a negative part and let the old satyr plot with the landlord to abduct *Manon*. *Des Grieux*, however, has seen her. "Donna non vidi mai simile a questa" (Never did I behold so fair a maiden), he sings in praise of her beauty.

With her too it is love at first sight. When she rejoins him, as she had promised to, they have a love duet. "Vedete! Io son fedele alla parola mia" (Behold me! I have been faithful to my promise), she sings. *Edmund*, who has overheard *Geronte's* plot to abduct *Manon*, informs *Des Grieux*, who has little trouble in inducing the girl to elope with him. They drive off in the carriage *Geronte* had ordered. *Lescaut*, who has been carousing with the students, hints that, as *Des Grieux* is not wealthy and *Manon* loves luxury, he will soon be able to persuade her to desert her lover for the rich Treasurer-General.

Such, indeed, is the case, and in Act II., she is found ensconced in luxurious apartments in *Geronte's* house in Paris. But to *Lescaut*, who prides himself on having brought the business with her wealthy admirer to a successful conclusion, she complains that "in quelle trine morbide"— in those silken curtains—there's a chill that freezes her. "O mia dimora umile, tu mi ritorni innanzi (My little humble dwelling, I see you there before me). She left *Des Grieux* for wealth and the luxuries it can bring—"Tell me, does not this gown suit me to perfection?" she asks *Lescaut* —and yet she longs for her handsome young lover.

Geronte sends singers to entertain her. They sing a madrigal, "Sulla vetta tu del monte erri, O Clori" (Speed o'er the summit of the mountain, gentle Chloe).

The Complete Opera Book

Then a dancing master enters. *Manon, Lescaut, Geronte,* and old beaus and abbés, who have come in with *Geronte,* form for the dance, and a lesson in the minuet begins.

Lescaut hurries off to inform *Des Grieux,* who has made money in gambling, where he can find *Manon.* When the lesson is over and all have gone, her lover appears at the door. At first he reproaches her, but soon is won by her beauty. There is an impassioned love duet, "Vieni! Colle tue braccia stringi Manon che t'ama" (Oh, come love! In your arms enfold Manon, who loves you).

Geronte surprises them, pretends to approve of their affection, but really sends for the police. *Lescaut* urges them to make a precipitate escape. *Manon,* however, now loathe to leave the luxuries *Geronte* has lavished on her, insists on gathering up her jewels in order to take them with her. The delay is fatal. The police arrive. She is arrested on the charge made by *Geronte* that she is an abandoned woman.

Her sentence is banishment, with other women of loose character, to the then French possession of Louisiana. The journey to Havre for embarkation is represented by an intermezzo in the score, and an extract from Abbé Prévost's story in the libretto. The theme of the "Intermezzo," a striking composition, is as follows:

Act III. The scene is laid in a square near the harbour at Havre. *Des Grieux* and *Lescaut* attempt to free

5

Giacomo Puccini

Manon from imprisonment, but are foiled. There is much hubbub. Then the roll is called of the women, who are to be transported. As they step forward, the crowd comments upon their looks. This, together with *Des Grieux's* plea to the captain of the ship to be taken along with *Manon*, no matter how lowly the capacity in which he may be required to serve on board, make a dramatic scene.

Act IV. "A vast plain on the borders of the territory of New Orleans. The country is bare and undulating, the horizon is far distant, the sky is overcast. Night falls." Thus the libretto. The score is a long, sad duet between *Des Grieux* and *Manon*. *Manon* dies of exhaustion. *Des Grieux* falls senseless upon her body.

LA BOHÈME

THE BOHEMIANS

Opera in four acts by Puccini; words by Giuseppe Giacosa and Luigi Illica, founded on Henri Murger's book, *La Vie de Bohème*. Produced, Teatro Reggio, Turin, February 1, 1896. Manchester, England, in English, as "The Bohemians," April 22, 1897. Covent Garden, London, in English, October 2, 1897; in Italian, July 1, 1899. San Francisco, March, 1898, and Wallack's Theatre, New York, May 16, 1898, by a second-rate travelling organization, which called itself The Milan Royal Italian Opera Company of La Scala; American Theatre, New York, in English, by Henry W. Savage's Castle Square Opera Company, November 20, 1898; Metropolitan Opera House, New York, in Italian, December 18, 1901.

CHARACTERS

RUDOLPH, a poet...*Tenor*
MARCEL, a painter.......................................*Baritone*
COLLINE, a philosopher..................................*Bass*
SCHAUNARD, a musician..................................*Baritone*
BENOIT, a landlord......................................*Bass*
ALCINDORO, a state councillor and follower of *Musetta*..........*Bass*
PARPIGNOL, an itinerant toy vender.....................*Tenor*
CUSTOM-HOUSE SERGEANT................................*Bass*
MUSETTA, a grisette.....................................*Soprano*

The Complete Opera Book

Mimi, a maker of embroidery.........................,....*Soprano*
Students, work girls, citizens, shopkeepers, street venders, soldiers, waiters, boys, girls, etc.
Time—About 1830.   *Place*—Latin Quarter, Paris.

"La Bohème" is considered by many Puccini's finest score. There is little to choose, however, between it, "Tosca," and "Madama Butterfly." Each deals successfully with its subject. It chances that, as "La Bohème" is laid in the Quartier Latin, the students' quarter of Paris, where gayety and pathos touch elbows, it laughs as well as weeps. Authors and composers who can tear passion to tatters are more numerous than those who have the light touch of high comedy. The latter, a distinguished gift, confers distinction upon many passages in the score of "La Bohème," which anon sparkles with merriment, anon is eloquent of love, anon is stressed by despair.

Act I. The garret in the Latin Quarter, where live the inseparable quartet—*Rudolph*, poet; *Marcel*, painter; *Colline*, philosopher; *Schaunard*, musician, who defy hunger with cheerfulness and play pranks upon the landlord of their meagre lodging, when he importunes them for his rent.

When the act opens, *Rudolph* is at a table writing, and *Marcel* is at work on a painting, "The Passage of the Red Sea." He remarks that, owing to lack of fuel for the garret stove, the Red Sea is rather cold.

"Questo mar rosso" (This Red Sea), runs the duet, in the course of which *Rudolph* says that he will sacrifice the manuscript of his tragedy to the needs of the stove. They tear up the first act, throw it into the stove, and light it. *Colline* comes in with a bundle of books he has vainly been attempting to pawn. Another act of the tragedy goes into the fire, by which they warm themselves, still hungry.

But relief is nigh. Two boys enter. They bring provisions and fuel. After them comes *Schaunard*. He tosses money on the table. The boys leave. In vain *Schaunard* tries to tell his friends the ludicrous details of his three-days' musical engagement to an eccentric Englishman. It is enough for them that it has yielded fuel and food, and that some money is left over for the immediate future. Between their noise in stoking the stove and unpacking the provisions, *Schaunard* cannot make himself heard.

Rudolph locks the door. Then all go to the table and pour out wine. It is Christmas eve. *Schaunard* suggests that, when they have emptied their glasses, they repair to their favourite resort, the Café Momus, and dine. Agreed. Just then there is a knock. It is *Benoit*, their landlord, for the rent. They let him in and invite him to drink with them. The sight of the money on the table reassures him. He joins them. The wine loosens his tongue. He boasts of his conquests of women at shady resorts. The four friends feign indignation. What! He, a married man, engaged in such disreputable proceedings! They seize him, lift him to his feet, and eject him, locking the door after him.

The money on the table was earned by *Schaunard*, but, according to their custom, they divide it. Now, off for the Café Momus—that is, all but *Rudolph*, who will join them soon—when he has finished an article he has to write for a new journal, the *Beaver*. He stands on the landing with a lighted candle to aid the others in making their way down the rickety stairs.

With little that can be designated as set melody, there nevertheless has not been a dull moment in the music of these scenes. It has been brisk, merry and sparkling, in keeping with the careless gayety of the four dwellers in the garret.

Re-entering the room, and closing the door after him, *Rudolph* clears a space on the table for pens and paper, then sits down to write. Ideas are slow in coming. Moreover, at that moment, there is a timid knock at the door.

"Who's there?" he calls.

It is a woman's voice that says, hesitatingly, "Excuse me, my candle has gone out."
Rudolph runs to the door, and opens it. On the threshold stands a frail, appealingly attractive young woman. She has in one hand an extinguished candle, in the other a key. *Rudolph* bids her come in. She crosses the threshold. A woman of haunting sweetness in aspect and manner has entered Bohemia.

She lights her candle by his, but, as she is about to leave, the draught again extinguishes it. *Rudolph's* candle also is blown out, as he hastens to relight hers. The room is dark, save for the moonlight that, over the snow-clad roofs of Paris, steals in through the garret window. *Mimi* exclaims that she has dropped the key to the door of her room. They search for it. He finds it but slips it into his pocket. Guided by *Mimi's* voice and movements, he approaches. As she stoops, his hand meets hers. He clasps it.

"Che gelida manina" (How cold your hand), he exclaims with tender solicitude. "Let me warm it into life." He then tells her who he is, in what has become known as the "Racconto di Rodolfo" (Rudolph's Narrative), which, from the gentle and solicitous phrase, "Che gelida manina," followed by the proud exclamation, "Sono un poeta" (I am a poet), leads up to an eloquent avowal of his dreams and fancies. Then comes the girl's charming "Mi chiamano Mimi" (They call me Mimi), in which she tells of her work and how the flowers she embroiders for a living transport her from her narrow room out into the broad fields and meadows. "Mi chiamano Mimi" is as follows:—

Giacomo Puccini

Her frailty, which one can see is caused by consumption in its early stages, makes her beauty the more appealing to *Rudolph.*

His friends call him from the street below. Their voices draw *Mimi* to the window. In the moonlight she appears even lovelier to *Rudolph.* "O soave fanciulla" (Thou beauteous maiden), he exclaims, as he takes her to his arms. This is the beginning of the love duet, which, though it be sung in a garret, is as impassioned as any that, in opera, has echoed through the corridors of palaces, or the moonlit colonnades of forests by historic rivers. The theme is quoted here in the key, in which it occurs, like a premonition, a little earlier in the act.

The theme of the love duet is used by the composer several times in the course of the opera, and always in association with *Mimi.* Especially in the last act does it recur with poignant effect.

Act II. A meeting of streets, where they form a square, with shops of all sorts, and the Café Momus. The square is filled with a happy Christmas eve crowd. Somewhat aloof from this are *Rudolph* and *Mimi.* *Colline* stands near the shop of a clothes dealer. *Schaunard* is haggling with a tinsmith over the price of a horn. *Marcel* is chaffing the girls who jostle against him in the crowd.

There are street venders crying their wares; citizens, students, and work girls, passing to and fro and calling to each other; people at the café giving orders—a merry whirl, depicted in the music by snatches of chorus, bits of recitative, and an instrumental accompaniment that runs through the scene like a many-coloured thread, and holds the pattern together. .

Rudolph and *Mimi* enter a bonnet shop. The animation outside continues. When the two lovers come out of the shop, *Mimi* is wearing a new bonnet trimmed with roses. She looks about.

"What is it?" *Rudolph* asks suspiciously.

"Are you jealous?" asks *Mimi*.

"The man in love is always jealous."

Rudolph's friends are at a table outside the café. *Rudolph* joins them with *Mimi*. He introduces her to them as one who will make their party complete, for he "will play the poet, while she's the muse incarnate."

Parpignol, the toy vender, crosses the square and goes off, followed by children, whose mothers try to restrain them. The toy vender is heard crying his wares in the distance. The quartet of Bohemians, now a quintet through the accession of *Mimi*, order eatables and wine.

Shopwomen, who are going away, look down one of the streets, and exclaim over some one whom they see approaching.

"'Tis Musetta! My, she is gorgeous!—Some stammering old dotard is with her."

Musetta and *Marcel* have loved, quarrelled, and parted. She has recently put up with the aged but wealthy *Alcindoro de Mittoneaux*, who, when she comes upon the square, is out of breath trying to keep up with her.

Despite *Musetta's* and *Marcel's* attempt to appear indifferent to each other's presence, it is plain that they are not so. *Musetta* has a chic waltz song, "Quando me 'n vo soletta per la via" (As through the streets I wander onward merrily), one of the best known numbers of the score, which she deliberately sings at *Marcel*, to make him aware, without arousing her aged gallant's suspicions, that she still loves him.

Giacomo Puccini

Feigning that a shoe hurts her, she makes the ridiculous
Alcindoro unlatch and remove it, and trot off with it to the
cobbler's. She and *Marcel* then embrace, and she joins
the five friends at their table, and the expensive supper
ordered by *Alcindoro* is served to them with their own.

The military tattoo is heard approaching from the distance. There is great confusion in the square. A waiter
brings the bill for the Bohemians' order. *Schaunard* looks
in vain for his purse. *Musetta* comes to the rescue. "Make
one bill of the two orders. The gentleman who was with
me will pay it."

The patrol enters, headed by a drum major. *Musetta*,
being without her shoe, cannot walk, so *Marcel* and *Colline*
lift her between them to their shoulders, and carry her
through the crowd, which, sensing the humour of the situation, gives her an ovation, then swirls around *Alcindoro*,
whose foolish, senile figure, appearing from the direction
of the cobbler's shop with a pair of shoes for *Musetta*, it
greets with jeers. For his gay ladybird has fled with her
friends from the *Quartier*, and left him to pay all the bills.

Act III. A gate to the city of Paris on the Orleans road.
A toll house at the gate. To the left a tavern, from which,
as a signboard hangs *Marcel's* picture of the Red Sea. Several
plane trees. It is February. Snow is on the ground.
The hour is that of dawn. Scavengers, milk women, truck-
men, peasants with produce, are waiting to be admitted
to the city. Custom-house officers are seated, asleep,
around a brazier. Sounds of revelry are heard from the
tavern. These, together with characteristic phrases, when

the gate is opened and people enter, enliven the first scene. Into the small square comes *Mimi* from the Rue d'Enfer, which leads from the Latin Quarter. She looks pale, distressed, and frailer than ever. A cough racks her. Now and then she leans against one of the bare, gaunt plane trees for support.

A message from her brings *Marcel* out of the tavern. He tells her he finds it more lucrative to paint signboards than pictures. *Musetta* gives music lessons. *Rudolph* is with them. Will not *Mimi* join them? She weeps, and tells him that *Rudolph* is so jealous of her she fears they must part. When *Rudolph*, having missed *Marcel*, comes out to look for him, *Mimi* hides behind a plane tree, from where she hears her lover tell his friend that he wishes to give her up because of their frequent quarrels. "Mimi è una civetta" (Mimi is a heartless creature) is the burden of his song. Her violent coughing reveals her presence. They decide to part—not angrily, but regretfully: "Addio, senza rancore" (Farewell, then, I wish you well), sings *Mimi*.

Meanwhile *Marcel*, who has re-entered the tavern, has caught *Musetta* flirting with a stranger. This starts a quarrel, which brings them out into the street. Thus the music becomes a quartet: "Addio, dolce svegliare" (Farewell, sweet love), sing *Rudolph* and *Mimi*, while *Marcel* and *Musetta* upbraid each other. The temperamental difference between the two women, *Mimi* gentle and melancholy, *Musetta* aggressive and disputatious, and the difference in the effect upon the two men, are admirably brought out by the composer. "Viper!" "Toad!" *Marcel* and

Giacomo Puccini

Musetta call out to each other, as they separate; while the frail *Mimi* sighs, "Ah! that our winter night might last forever," and she and *Rudolph* sing, "Our time for parting's when the roses blow."

Act IV. The scene is again the attic of the four Bohemians. *Rudolph* is longing for *Mimi*, of whom he has heard nothing, *Marcel* for *Musetta*, who, having left him, is indulging in one of her gay intermezzos with one of her wealthy patrons. "Ah, Mimi, tu piu" (Ah, Mimi, fickle-hearted), sings *Rudolph*, as he gazes at the little pink bonnet he bought her at the milliner's shop Christmas eve. *Schaunard* thrusts the water bottle into *Colline's* hat as if the latter were a champagne cooler. The four friends seek to forget sorrow and poverty in assuming mock dignities and then indulging in a frolic about the attic. When the fun is at its height, the door opens and *Musetta* enters. She announces that *Mimi* is dying and, as a last request, has asked to be brought back to the attic, where she had been so happy with *Rudolph*. He rushes out to get her, and supports her feeble and faltering footsteps to the cot, on which he gently lowers her.

She coughs; her hands are very cold. *Rudolph* takes them in his to warm them. *Musetta* hands her earrings to *Marcel*, and bids him go out and sell them quickly, then buy a tonic for the dying girl. There is no coffee, no wine. *Colline* takes off his overcoat, and, having apostrophized it in the "Song of the Coat," goes out to sell it, so as to be able to replenish the larder. *Musetta* runs off to get her muff for *Mimi*, her hands are still so cold.

Rudolph and the dying girl are now alone. This tragic moment, when their love revives too late, finds expression, at once passionate and exquisite, in the music. The phrases "How cold your hand," "They call me Mimi," from the love scene in the first act, recur like mournful memories.

14

The Complete Opera Book

Mimi whispers of incidents from early in their love. "Te lo rammenti" (Ah! do you remember).

Musetta and the others return. There are tender touches in the good offices they would render the dying girl. They are aware before *Rudolph* that she is beyond aid. In their faces he reads what has happened. With a cry, "Mimi! Mimi!" he falls sobbing upon her lifeless form. *Musetta* kneels weeping at the foot of the bed. *Schaunard*, overcome sinks back into a chair. *Colline* stands dazed at the suddenness of the catastrophe. *Marcel* turns away to hide his emotion.

Mi chiamano Mimi!

TOSCA

Opera in three acts by Puccini; words by L. Illica and G. Giacosa after the drama, "La Tosca," by Sardou. Produced, Constanzi Theatre, Rome, January 14, 1900; London, Covent Garden, July 12, 1900. Buenos Aires, June 16, 1900. Metropolitan Opera House, New York, February 4, 1901, with Ternina, Cremonini, Scotti, Gilibert (*Sacristan*), and Dufriche (*Angelotti*).

CHARACTERS

FLORIA TOSCA, a celebrated singer.......................*Soprano*
MARIO CAVARADOSSI, a painter...........................*Tenor*
BARON SCARPIA, Chief of Police........................*Baritone*

Giacomo Puccini

Three sharp, vigorous chords, denoting the imperious yet sinister and vindictive character of *Scarpia*—such is the introduction to "Tosca."

Act I. The church of Sant' Andrea alla Valle. To the right the Attavanti chapel; left a scaffolding, dais, and easel. On the easel a large picture covered by a cloth. Painting accessories. A basket.

Enter *Angelotti*. He has escaped from prison and is seeking a hiding place. Looking about, he recognizes a pillar shrine containing an image of the Virgin, and surmounting a receptacle for holy water. Beneath the feet of the image he searches for and discovers a key, unlocks the Attavanti chapel and disappears within it. The *Sacristan* comes in. He has a bunch of brushes that he has been cleaning, and evidently is surprised not to find *Cavaradossi* at his easel. He looks into the basket, finds the luncheon in it untouched, and now is sure he was mistaken in thinking he had seen the painter enter.

The Angelus is rung. The *Sacristan* kneels. *Cavaradossi* enters. He uncovers the painting—a Mary Magdalen with large blue eyes and masses of golden hair. The *Sacristan* recognizes in it the portrait of a lady who lately has come frequently to the church to worship. The good man is scandalized at what he considers a sacrilege. *Cavaradossi*, however, has other things to think of. He compares the face in the portrait with the features of the woman he loves, the dark-eyed *Floria Tosca*, famous as a singer. "Recondita armonia di bellezza diverse" (Strange harmony of contrasts deliciously blending), he sings.

Meanwhile the *Sacristan*, engaged in cleaning the brushes in a jug of water, continues to growl over the sacrilege of putting frivolous women into religious paintings. Finally, his task with the brushes over, he points to the basket and asks, "Are you fasting?" "Nothing for me," says the painter. The *Sacristan* casts a greedy look at the basket, as he thinks of the benefit he will derive from the artist's abstemiousness. The painter goes on with his work. The *Sacristan* leaves.

Angelotti, believing no one to be in the church, comes out of his hiding place. He and *Cavaradossi* recognize each other. *Angelotti* has just escaped from the prison in the castle of Sant' Angelo. The painter at once offers to help him. Just then, however, *Tosca's* voice is heard outside. The painter presses the basket with wine and viands upon the exhausted fugitive, and urges him back into the chapel, while from without *Tosca* calls more insistently, "Mario!"

Feigning calm, for the meeting with *Angelotti*, who had been concerned in the abortive uprising to make Rome a republic, has excited him, *Cavaradossi* admits *Tosca*. Jealously she insists that he was whispering with some one, and that she heard footsteps and the swish of skirts. Her lover reassures her, tries to embrace her. Gently she reproves him. She cannot let him kiss her before the Madonna until she has prayed to her image and made an offering. She adorns the Virgin's figure with flowers she has brought with her, kneels in prayer, crosses herself and rises. She tells *Cavaradossi* to await her at the stage door that night, and they will steal away together to his villa. He is still distrait. When he replies, absent-mindedly, he surely will be there, her comment is, "Thou say'st it badly." Then, beginning the love duet, "Non, la sospiri la nostra

17

EMMA EAMES AS TOSCA.

SCOTTI AS SCARPIA.

Giacomo Puccini

casetta" (Dost thou not long for our dovecote secluded), she conjures up for him a vision of that "sweet, sweet nest in which we love-birds hide."

For the moment *Cavaradossi* forgets *Angelotti;* then, however, urges *Tosca* to leave him, so that he may continue with his work. She is vexed and, when she recognizes in the picture of Mary Magdalen the fair features of the Marchioness Attavanti, she becomes jealous to the point of rage. But her lover soon soothes her. The episode is charming. In fact the libretto, following the Sardou play, unfolds, scene by scene, an always effective drama.

Tosca having departed, *Cavaradossi* lets *Angelotti* out of the chapel. He is a brother of the Attavanti, of whom *Tosca* is so needlessly jealous, and who has concealed a suit of woman's clothing for him under the altar. They mention *Scarpia*—"A bigoted satyr and hypocrite, secretly steeped in vice, yet most demonstratively pious"—the first hint we have in the opera of the relentless character, whose desire to possess *Tosca* is the mainspring of the drama.

A cannon shot startles them. It is from the direction of the castle and announces the escape of a prisoner—*Angelotti*. *Cavaradossi* suggests the grounds of his villa as a place of concealment from *Scarpia* and his police agents, especially the old dried-up well, from which a secret passage leads to a dark vault. It can be reached by a rough path just outside the Attavanti chapel. The painter even offers to guide the fugitive. They leave hastily.

The *Sacristan* enters excitedly. He has great news. Word has been received that Bonaparte has been defeated. The old man now notices, however, greatly to his surprise, that the painter has gone. Acolytes, penitents, choristers, and pupils of the chapel crowd in from all directions. There is to be a "Te Deum" in honour of the victory, and at evening, in the Farnese palace, a cantata with *Floria Tosca*

as soloist. It means extra pay for the choristers. They
are jubilant.

Scarpia enters unexpectedly. He stands in a doorway.
A sudden hush falls upon all. For a while they are motionless, as if spellbound. While preparations are making
for the "Te Deum," *Scarpia* orders search made in the
Attavanti chapel. He finds a fan which, from the coat-
of-arms on it, he recognizes as having been left there by *Angelotti's* sister. A police agent also finds a basket. As he
comes out with it, the *Sacristan* unwittingly exclaims that
it is *Cavaradossi's*, and empty, although the painter had
said that he would eat nothing. It is plain to *Scarpia*, who
has also discovered in the Mary Magdalen of the picture
the likeness to the Marchioness Attavanti, that *Cavaradossi*
had given the basket of provisions to *Angelotti*, and has been
an accomplice in his escape.

Tosca comes in and quickly approaches the dais. She is
greatly surprised not to find *Cavaradossi* at work on the
picture. *Scarpia* dips his fingers in holy water and deferentially extends them to *Tosca*. Reluctantly she touches
them, then crosses herself. *Scarpia* insinuatingly compli-
ments her on her religious zeal. She comes to church to
pray, not, like certain frivolous wantons—he points to the
picture—to meet their lovers. He now produces the fan.
"Is this a painter's brush or a mahlstick?" he asks, and
adds that he found it on the easel. Quickly, jealously,
Tosca examines it, sees the arms of the Attavanti. She
had come to tell her lover that, because she is obliged to
sing in the cantata she will be unable to meet him that
night. Her reward is this evidence, offered by *Scarpia*,
that he has been carrying on a love affair with another
woman, with whom he probably has gone to the villa.
She gives way to an outburst of jealous rage; then, weeping,
leaves the chapel, to the gates of which *Scarpia* gallantly
escorts her. He beckons to his agent *Spoletta*, and orders

Giacomo Puccini

him to trail her and report to him at evening at the Farnese palace.

Church bells are tolling. Intermittently, from the castle of Sant' Angelo comes the boom of the cannon. A Cardinal has entered and is advancing to the high altar. The "Te Deum" has begun. *Scarpia* soliloquizes vindictively: "Va, Tosca! Nel tuo cuor s'annida Scarpia" (Go, Tosca! There is room in your heart for Scarpia).

He pauses to bow reverently as the Cardinal passes by. Still soliloquizing, he exults in his power to send *Cavaradossi* to execution, while *Tosca* he will bring to his own arms. For her, he exclaims, he would renounce his hopes of heaven; then kneels and fervently joins in the "Te Deum."

This finale, with its elaborate apparatus, its complex emotions and the sinister and dominating figure of *Scarpia* set against a brilliant and constantly shifting background, is a stirring and effective climax to the act.

Act II. The Farnese Palace. *Scarpia's* apartments on an upper floor. A large window overlooks the palace courtyard. *Scarpia* is seated at table supping. At intervals he breaks off to reflect. His manner is anxious. An orchestra is heard from a lower story of the palace, where Queen Caroline is giving an entertainment in honour of the reported victory over Bonaparte. They are dancing, while waiting for *Tosca*, who is to sing in the cantata. *Scarpia* summons *Sciarrone* and gives him a letter, which is to be handed to the singer upon her arrival.

Spoletta returns from his mission. *Tosca* was followed to a villa almost hidden by foliage. She remained but a short time. When she left it, *Spoletta* and his men searched the house, but could not find *Angelotti*. *Scarpia* is furious, but is appeased when *Spoletta* tells him that they discovered *Cavaradossi*, put him in irons, and have brought him with them.

Through the open window there is now heard the beginning of the cantata, showing that *Tosca* has arrived and is on the floor below, where are the Queen's reception rooms. Upon *Scarpia's* order there are brought in *Cavaradossi*, *Roberti*, the executioner, and a judge with his clerk. *Cavaradossi's* manner is indignant, defiant. *Scarpia's* at first suave. Now and then *Tosca's* voice is heard singing below. Finally *Scarpia* closes the window, thus shutting out the music. His questions addressed to *Cavaradossi* are now put in a voice more severe. He has just asked, "Once more and for the last time," where is *Angelotti*, when *Tosca*, evidently alarmed by the contents of the note received from *Scarpia*, hurries in and, seeing *Cavaradossi*, fervently embraces him. Under his breath he manages to warn her against disclosing anything she saw at the villa.

Scarpia orders that *Cavaradossi* be removed to an adjoining room and his deposition there taken. *Tosca* is not aware that it is the torture chamber the door to which has closed upon her lover. With *Tosca Scarpia* begins his interview quietly, deferentially. He has deduced from *Spoletta's* report of her having remained but a short time at the villa that, instead of discovering the Attavanti with her lover, as she jealously had suspected, she had found him making plans to conceal *Angelotti*. In this he has just been confirmed by her frankly affectionate manner toward *Cavaradossi*.

At first she answers *Scarpia's* questions as to the presence of someone else at the villa lightly; then, when he becomes more insistent, her replies show irritation, until, turning on her with "ferocious sternness," he tells her that his agents are attempting to wring a confession from *Cavaradossi* by torture. ‚Even at that moment a groan is heard. *Tosca* implores mercy for her lover. Yes, if she will disclose the hiding place of *Angelotti*. Groan after groan escapes from the torture chamber. *Tosca*, overcome, bursts into convulsive sobs and sinks back upon a sofa. *Spoletta* kneels

Giacomo Puccini

and mutters a Latin prayer. ' *Scarpia* remains cruelly impassive, silent, until, seeing his opportunity in *Tosca's* collapse, he steps to the door and signals to the executioner, *Roberti*, to apply still greater torture. The air is rent with a prolonged cry of pain. Unable longer to bear her lover's anguish and, in spite of warnings to say nothing, which he has called out to her between his spasms, she says hurriedly and in a stifled voice to *Scarpia*, "The well . . . in the garden."

Cavaradossi is borne in from the torture chamber and deposited on the sofa. Kneeling beside him *Tosca* lavishes tears and kisses upon him. *Sciarrone*, the judge, *Roberti* and the *Clerk* go. In obedience to a sign from *Scarpia*, *Spoletta* and the agents remain behind. Still loyal to his friend, *Cavaradossi*, although racked with pain, asks *Tosca* if unwittingly in his anguish he has disclosed aught. She reassures him.

In a loud and commanding voice *Scarpia* says to *Spoletta:* "In the well in the garden—Go *Spoletta!*"

From *Scarpia's* words *Cavaradossi* knows that *Tosca* has betrayed *Angelotti's* hiding place. He tries to repulse her.

Sciarrone rushes in much perturbed. He brings bad news. The victory they have been celebrating has turned into defeat. Bonaparte has triumphed at Marengo. *Cavaradossi* is roused to enthusiasm by the tidings. "Tremble, Scarpia, thou butcherly hypocrite," he cries.

It is his death warrant. At *Scarpia's* command *Sciarrone* and the agents seize him and drag him away to be hanged.

Quietly seating himself at table, *Scarpia* invites *Tosca* to a chair. Perhaps they can discover a plan by which *Cavaradossi* may be saved. He carefully polishes a wineglass with a napkin, fills it with wine, and pushes it toward her.

"Your price?" she asks, contemptuously.

Imperturbably he fills his glass. She is the price that

must be paid for *Cavaradossi's* life. The horror with which she shrinks from the proposal, her unfeigned detestation of the man putting it forward, make her seem the more fascinating to him. There is a sound of distant drums. It is the escort that will conduct *Cavaradossi* to the scaffold. *Scarpia* has almost finished supper. Imperturbably he peels an apple and cuts it in quarters, occasionally looking up and scanning his chosen victim's features.

Distracted, not knowing whither or to whom to turn, *Tosca* now utters the famous "Vissi d'arte e d'amor, non feci ma male ad anima viva":

> (Music and love—these have I lived for,
> Nor ever have I harmed a living being . . .
>
> . . . .
>
> In this, my hour of grief and bitter tribulation,
> O, Heavenly Father, why hast Thou forsaken me),

The "Vissi d'arte" justly is considered the most beautiful air in the repertoire of modern Italian opera. It is to passages of surpassing eloquence like this that Puccini owes his fame, and his operas are indebted for their lasting power of appeal.

Beginning quietly, "Vissi d'arte e d'amor," it works

up to the impassioned, heart-rending outburst of grief with which it comes to an end.

CAVALIERI AS TOSCA.

CARUSO AS MARIO IN "TOSCA."

Giacomo Puccini

A knock at the door. *Spoletta* comes to announce that *Angelotti*, on finding himself discovered, swallowed poison. "The other," he adds, meaning *Cavaradossi*, "awaits your decision." The life of *Tosca's* lover is in the hands of the man who has told her how she may save him. Softly *Scarpia* asks her, "What say you?" She nods consent; then, weeping for the shame of it, buries her head in the sofa cushions.

Scarpia says it is necessary for a mock execution to be gone through with, before *Tosca* and *Cavaradossi* can flee Rome. He directs *Spoletta* that the execution is to be simulated—"as we did in the case of Palmieri.—You understand."

"Just like Palmieri," *Spoletta* repeats with emphasis, and goes.

Scarpia turns to *Tosca*. "I have kept my promise " She, however, demands safe conduct for *Cavaradossi* and herself. *Scarpia* goes to his desk to write the paper. With trembling hand *Tosca*, standing at the table, raises to her lips the wineglass filled for her by *Scarpia*. As she does so she sees the sharp, pointed knife with which he peeled and quartered the apple. A rapid glance at the desk assures her that he still is writing. With infinite caution she reaches out, secures possession of the knife, conceals it on her person. *Scarpia* has finished writing. He folds up the paper, advances toward *Tosca* with open arms to embrace her.

"*Tosca*, at last thou art mine!"

With a swift stroke of the knife, she stabs him full in the breast.

"It is thus that *Tosca* kisses!"

He staggers, falls. Ineffectually he strives to rise; makes a final effort; falls backward; dies.

Glancing back from time to time at *Scarpia's* corpse, *Tosca* goes to the table, where she dips a napkin in water and washes her fingers. She arranges her hair before a looking-glass, then looks on the desk for the safe-conduct. Not finding it there, she searches elsewhere for it, finally discovers it clutched in *Scarpia's* dead fingers, lifts his arm, draws out the paper from between the fingers, and lets the arm fall back stiff and stark, as she hides the paper in her bosom. For a brief moment she surveys the body, then extinguishes the lights on the supper table.

About to leave, she sees one of the candles on the desk still burning. With a grace of solemnity, she lights with it the other candle, places one candle to the right, the other to the left of *Scarpia's* head, takes down a crucifix from the wall, and, kneeling, places it on the dead man's breast. There is a roll of distant drums. She rises; steals out of the room.

In the opera, as in the play, which was one of Sarah Bernhardt's triumphs, it is a wonderful scene—one of the greatest in all drama. Anyone who has seen it adequately acted, knows what it has signified in the success of the opera, even after giving Puccini credit for "Vissi d'arte" and an expressive accompaniment to all that transpires on the stage.

Act III. A platform of the Castle Sant' Angelo. Left, a casement with a table, a bench, and a stool. On the table are a lantern, a huge register book, and writing materials. Suspended on one of the walls are a crucifix and a votive lamp. Right, a trap door opening on a flight of steps that lead to the platform from below. The Vatican and St. Paul's are seen in the distance. The clear sky is studded with stars. It is just before dawn. The jangle of sheep bells is heard, at first distant, then nearer. Without, a shepherd sings his lay. A dim, grey light heralds the approach of dawn.

The firing party conducting *Cavaradossi* ascends the steps through the trap door and is received by a jailer. From a paper handed him by the sergeant in charge of the picket, the jailer makes entries in the register, to which the sergeant signs his name, then descends the steps followed by the picket. A bell strikes. "You have an hour," the jailer tells *Cavaradossi*. The latter craves the favour of being permitted to write a letter. It being granted, he begins to write, but soon loses himself in memories of *Tosca*. "E lucevan le stelle ed olezzava la terra" (When the stars were brightly shining, and faint perfumes the air pervaded)—a tenor air of great beauty.

He buries his face in his hands. *Spoletta* and the sergeant conduct *Tosca* up the steps to the platform, and point out to her where she will find *Cavaradossi*. A dim light still envelopes the scene as with mystery. *Tosca*, seeing her lover, rushes up to him and, unable to speak for sheer emotion, lifts his hands and shows him—herself and the safe-conduct.

"At what price?" he asks.

Swiftly she tells him what *Scarpia* demanded of her, and how, having consented, she thwarted him by slaying him with her own hand. Lovingly he takes her hands in his. "O dolci mani mansuede e pure" (Oh! gentle hands, so pitiful and tender). Her voice mingles with his in love and gratitude for deliverance.

Amaro sol per te m'era il morire " (The sting of death, I only felt for thee, love).

She informs him of the necessity of going through a mock execution. He must fall naturally and lie perfectly still, as if dead, until she calls to him. They laugh over the ruse. It will be amusing. The firing party arrives. The sergeant offers to bandage *Cavaradossi's* eyes. The latter declines. He stands with his back to the wall. The soldiers take aim. *Tosca* stops her ears with her hands so that she may not hear the explosion. The officer lowers his sword. The soldiers fire. *Cavaradossi* falls.

"How well he acts it!" exclaims *Tosca*.

A cloth is thrown over *Cavaradossi*. The firing party marches off. *Tosca* cautions her lover not to move yet. The footsteps of the firing party die away—"Now get up." He does not move. Can he not hear? She goes nearer to him. "Mario! Up quickly! Away!—Up! up! Mario!"

She raises the cloth. To the last *Scarpia* has tricked her. He had ordered a real, not a mock execution. Her lover lies at her feet—a corpse.

There are cries from below the platform. *Scarpia's* murder has been discovered. His myrmidons are hastening to apprehend her. She springs upon the parapet and throws herself into space.

MADAMA BUTTERFLY

MADAM BUTTERFLY

Opera in two acts, by Giacomo Puccini, words after the story of John Luther Long and the drama of David Belasco by L. Illica and G. Giacosa. English version by Mrs. R. H. Elkin. Produced unsuccessfully,

Giacomo Puccini

La Scala, Milan, February 17, 1904, with Storchio, Zenatello, and De Luca, conductor Cleofante Campanini. Slightly revised, but with Act II. divided into two distinct parts, at Brescia, May 28, 1904, with Krusceniski, Zenatello, and Bellati; when it scored a success. Covent Garden, London, July 10, 1905, with Destinn, Caruso, and Scotti, conductor Campanini. Washington, D. C., October, 1906, in English, by the Savage Opera Company, and by the same company,Garden Theatre, New York, November 12, 1906, with Elsa Szamozy, Harriet Behne, Joseph F. Sheehan, and Winifred Goff; Metropolitan Opera House, New York, February 11, 1907, with Farrar (*Butterfly*), Homer (*Suzuki*), Caruso (*Pinkerton*), Scotti (*Sharpless*), and Reiss (*Goro*).

CHARACTERS

MADAM BUTTERFLY (Cio-Cio-San)....................*Soprano*
SUZUKI (her servant)..............................*Mezzo-Soprano*
KATE PINKERTON....................................*Mezzo-Soprano*
B. F. PINKERTON, Lieutenant, U. S. N..............*Tenor*
SHARPLESS (U. S. Consul at Nagasaki)..............*Baritone*
GORO (a marriage broker)..........................*Tenor*
PRINCE YAMADORI...................................*Baritone*
THE BONZE (*Cio-Cio-San's uncle*).................*Bass*
YAKUSIDE..*Baritone*
THE IMPERIAL COMMISSIONER.........................*Bass*
THE OFFICIAL REGISTRA ⎞ ....*Baritone*
CIO-CIO-SAN'S MOTHER ⎟ Members of.............*Mezzo-Soprano*
THE AUNT ⎟ the Chorus.............*Mezzo-Soprano*
THE COUSIN ⎠ ....*Soprano*
TROUBLE (*Cio-Cio-San's Child*)....................
Cio-Cio-San's relations and friends. Servants.

Time—Present day.   *Place*—Nagasaki.

Although "Madama Butterfly" is in two acts, the division of the second act into two parts by the fall of the curtain, there also being an instrumental introduction to part second, practically gives the opera three acts.

Act I. There is a prelude, based on a Japanese theme. This theme runs through the greater part of the act. It is employed as a background and as a connecting link, with the result that it imparts much exotic tone colour to the scenes. The prelude passes over into the first act without a break.

Lieutenant B. F. Pinkerton, U. S. N., is on the point of contracting a "Japanese marriage" with *Cio-Cio-San*, whom her friends call *Butterfly*. At the rise of the curtain *Pinkerton* is looking over a little house on a hill facing the harbour. This house he has leased and is about to occupy with his Japanese wife. *Goro*, the nakodo or marriage broker, who has arranged the match, also has found the house for him and is showing him over it, enjoying the American's surprise at the clever contrivances found in Japanese house construction. Three Japanese servants are in the house, one of whom is *Suzuki*, *Butterfly's* faithful maid.

Sharpless, the American Consul at Nagasaki, arrives. In the chat which follows between the two men it becomes apparent that *Sharpless* looks upon the step *Pinkerton* is about to take with disfavour. He argues that what may be a mere matter of pastime to the American Naval lieutenant, may have been taken seriously by the Japanese girl and, if so, may prove a matter of life or death with her. *Pinkerton* on the other hand laughs off his friend's fears and, having poured out drinks for both, recklessly pledges his real American wife of the future. Further discussion is interrupted by the arrival of the bride with her relatives and friends.

After greetings have been exchanged, the *Consul* on conversing with *Butterfly* becomes thoroughly convinced that he was correct in cautioning *Pinkerton*. For he discovers that she is not contemplating the usual Japanese marriage of arrangement, but, actually being in love with *Pinkerton*, is taking it with complete seriousness. She has even gone to the extent, as she confides to *Pinkerton*, of secretly renouncing her religious faith, the faith of her forefathers, and embracing his, before entering on her new life

[Dover Street Studios

DESTINN IN "MADAME BUTTERFLY."

ROSINA BUCKMAN IN "MADAME BUTTERFLY."

Giacomo Puccini

with him. This step, when discovered by her relatives, means that she has cut herself loose from all her old associations and belongings, and entrusts herself and her future entirely to her husband.

Minor officials whose duty it is to see that the marriage contract, even though it be a "Japanese marriage," is signed with proper ceremony, arrive. In the midst of drinking and merry-making on the part of all who have come to the wedding, they are startled by fierce imprecations from a distance and gradually drawing nearer. A weird figure, shouting and cursing wildly, appears upon the scene. It is *Butterfly's* uncle, the *Bonze* (Japanese priest). He has discovered her renunciation of faith, now calls down curses upon her head for it, and insists that all her relatives, even her immediate family, renounce her. *Pinkerton* enraged at the disturbance turns them out of the house. The air shakes with their imprecations as they depart. *Butterfly* is weeping bitterly, but *Pinkerton* soon is enabled to comfort her. The act closes with a passionate love scene.

The Japanese theme, which I have spoken of as forming the introduction to the act, besides, the background to the greater part of it, in fact up to the scene with the *Bonze*, never becomes monotonous because it is interrupted by several other musical episodes. Such are the short theme to which *Pinkerton* sings "Tutto e Pronto" (All is ready), and the skippy little theme when *Goro* tells *Pinkerton* about those who will be present at the ceremony. When *Pinkerton* sings, "The whole world over, on business or pleasure the Yankee travels," a motif based on the "Star Spangled Banner," is heard for the first time.

In the duet between *Pinkerton* and *Sharpless*, which *Pinkerton* begins with the words, "Amore o grillo" (Love or fancy), *Sharpless's* serious argument and its suggestion of the possibility of *Butterfly's* genuine love for *Pinkerton* are well brought out in the music. When *Butterfly* and her party arrive, her voice soars above those of the others to the strains of the same theme which occurs as a climax to the love duet at the end of the act and which, in the course of the opera, is heard on other occasions so intimately associated with herself and her emotions that it may be regarded as a motif, expressing the love she has conceived for *Pinkerton*.

Full of feeling is the music of her confession to *Pinkerton* that she has renounced the faith of her forefathers, in order to be a fit wife for the man she loves:—"Ieri son salita" (Hear what I would tell you). An episode, brief but of great charm, is the chorus "Kami! O Kami! Let's drink to the newly married couple." Then comes the interruption of the cheerful scene by the appearance of the *Bonze*, which forms a dramatic contrast.

It is customary with Puccini to create "atmosphere" of time and place through the medium of the early scenes of his operas. It is only necessary to recall the opening episodes in the first acts of "La Bohème" and "Tosca." He has done the same thing in "Madam Butterfly," by the employment of the Japanese theme already referred to, and by the crowded episodes attending the arrival of *Butterfly* and the performance of the ceremony. These episodes are full of action and colour, and distinctly Japanese in the impression they make. Moreover, they afford the only opportunity throughout the entire opera to employ the chorus upon the open stage. It is heard again in the second act, but only behind the scenes and humming in order to give the effect of distance.

The love scene between *Pinkerton* and *Butterfly* is extended. From its beginning, "Viene la sera" (Evening is falling),

to the end, its interest never flags. It is full of beautiful melody charged with sentiment and passion, yet varied with lighter passages, like *Butterfly's* "I am like the moon's little goddess"; "I used to think if anyone should want me"; and the exquisite, "Vogliatemi bene" (Ah, love me a little). There is a beautiful melody for *Pinkerton*, "Love, what fear holds you trembling." The climax of the love duet is reached in two impassioned phrases:—"Dolce notte! Quante stelle" (Night of rapture, stars unnumbered),

and "Oh! Quanti occhi fisi, attenti" (Oh, kindly heavens).

Act II. Part I. Three years have elapsed. It is a long time since *Pinkerton* has left *Butterfly* with the promise to return to her "when the robins nest." When the curtain rises, after an introduction, in which another Japanese theme is employed, *Suzuki*, although convinced that *Pinkerton* has deserted her mistress, is praying for his return. *Butterfly* is full of faith and trust. In chiding her devoted maid for doubting that *Pinkerton* will return, she draws in language and song a vivid picture of his home-coming and of their mutual joy therein:—"Un bel di vedremo" (Some day he'll come).

In point of fact, *Pinkerton* really is returning to Nagasaki, but with no idea of resuming relations with his Japanese wife. Indeed, before leaving America he has written to *Sharpless* asking him to let *Butterfly* know that he is married to an American wife, who will join him in Nagasaki. *Sharpless* calls upon *Butterfly*, and attempts to deliver his message, but is unable to do so because of the emotions aroused in *Butterfly* by the very sight of a letter from *Pinkerton*. It throws her into a transport of joy because, unable immediately to grasp its contents, she believes that in writing he has remembered her, and must be returning to her. *Sharpless* endeavours to make the true situation clear to her, but is interrupted by a visit from *Yamadori*, a wealthy Japanese suitor, whom *Goro* urges *Butterfly* to marry. For the money left by Pinkerton with his little Japanese wife has dwindled almost to nothing, and poverty stares her in the face. But she will not hear of an alliance with *Yamadori*. She protests that she is already married to *Pinkerton*, and will await his return.

When *Yamadori* has gone, *Sharpless* makes one more effort to open her eyes to the truth. They have a duet, "Ora a noi" (Now at last), in which he again produces the letter, and attempts to persuade her that Pinkerton has been faithless to her and has forgotten her. Her only reply is to fetch in her baby boy, born since *Pinkerton's* departure. Her argument is, that when the boy's father hears what a fine son is waiting for him in Japan, he will hasten back. She sings to *Trouble*, as the little boy is called:—"Sai cos' ebbe cuore" (Do you hear, my sweet one, what that bad man is saying). *Sharpless* makes a final effort to disillusion her, but in vain. If *Pinkerton* does not come back, there are two things, she says, she can do—return to her old life and sing for people, or die. She sings a touching little lullaby to her baby boy, *Suzuki* twice interrupting her with the pathetically voiced exclamation, "Poor Madam Butterfly!"

A salute of cannon from the harbour announces the arrival of a man-of-war. Looking through the telescope, *Butterfly* and *Suzuki* discover that it is *Pinkerton's* ship, the "Abraham Lincoln." Now *Butterfly* is convinced that

Giacomo Puccini

Sharpless is wrong. Her faith is about to be rewarded. The man she loves is returning to her. The home must be decorated and made cheerful and attractive to greet him. She and *Suzuki* distribute cherry blossoms wherever their effect will be most charming. The music accompanying this is the enchanting duet of the flowers, "Scuotti quella fronda diciliegio" (Shake that cherry tree till every flower). Most effective is the phrase, "Gettiamo a mani piene mammole e tuberose" (In handfuls let us scatter violets and white roses.)

Butterfly adorns herself and the baby boy. Then with her fingers she pierces three holes in the paper wall of the dwelling. She, *Suzuki*, and the baby peer through these, watching for *Pinkerton's* arrival. Night falls. *Suzuki* and the boy drop off to sleep. *Butterfly* rigid, motionless, waits and watches, her faith still unshaken, for the return of the man who has forsaken her. The pathos of the scene is profound; the music, with the hum of voices, borne upon the night from the distant harbour, exquisite.

Act II. Part II. When the curtain rises, night has passed, dawn is breaking. *Suzuki* and the baby are fast asleep, but *Butterfly* still is watching. Again Puccini employs a Japanese melody (the "vigil" theme).

When *Suzuki* awakes, she persuades the poor little "wife" to go upstairs to rest, which *Butterfly* does only upon *Suzuki's* promise to awaken her as soon as *Pinkerton* arrives. *Pinkerton* and *Sharpless* appear. *Suzuki* at first is full of joyful surprise, which, however, soon gives way to consternation, when she learns the truth. *Pinkerton* himself, seeing about him the proofs of *Butterfly's* complete loyalty to him, realizes the heartlessness of his own conduct. There is a dramatic trio for *Pinkerton, Sharpless,* and *Suzuki*. *Pinkerton* who cannot bear to face the situation, rushes away, leaving it to *Sharpless* to settle matters as best he can.

Butterfly has become aware that people are below. *Suzuki* tries to prevent her coming down, but she appears radiantly happy, for she expects to find her husband. The pathos of the scene in which she learns the truth is difficult to describe. But she does not burst into lamentations. With a gentleness which has been characteristic of her throughout, she bears the blow. She even expresses the wish to *Kate, Pinkerton's* real wife, that she may experience all happiness, and sends word to *Pinkerton* that, if he will come for his son in half an hour, he can have him.

Sharpless and *Mrs. Pinkerton* withdraw. In a scene of tragic power, *Butterfly* mortally wounds herself with her father's sword, the blade of which bears the inscription, "To die with honour when one can no longer live with honour," drags herself across the floor to where the boy is playing with his toys and waving a little American flag, and expires just as *Pinkerton* enters to take away the son whom thus she gives up to him.

From examples that already have been given of modern Italian opera, it is clear that "atmosphere," local colour, and character delineation are typical features of the art of Italy's lyric stage as it flourishes today. In "Madama Butterfly" we have exotic tone colour to a degree that has been approached but not equalled by Verdi in "Aïda." Certain brief scenes in Verdi's opera are Egyptian in tone colour. In "Madama Butterfly" Japanese themes are used *in extenso*, and although the thrilling climaxes in the work are distinctively Italian, the Japanese under-current, dramatic and musical, always is felt. In that respect compare "Madama

Giacomo Puccini

Butterfly" with a typical old Italian opera like "Lucia di Lammermoor" the scene of which is laid in Scotland, but in which there is nothing Scotch save the costumes—no "atmosphere," no local colour. These things are taken seriously by modern Italian composers, who do not ignore melody, yet also appreciate the value of an eloquent instrumental support to the voice score; whereas the older Italian opera composers were content to distribute melody with a lavish hand and took little else into account.

In character delineation in the opera *Butterfly* dominates. She is a sweet, trusting, pathetic little creature—traits expressed in the music as clearly as in the drama. The sturdy devotion of *Suzuki* is, if possible, brought out in an even stronger light in the opera than in the drama, and *Sharpless* is admirably drawn. *Pinkerton*, of course, cannot be made sympathetic. All that can be expected of him is that he be a tenor, and sing the beautiful music allotted to him in the first act with tender and passionate expression.

The use of the "Star-Spangled Banner" motif as a personal theme for *Pinkerton*, always has had a disagreeable effect upon me, and from now on should be objected to by all Americans. Some one in authority, a manager like Gatti-Casazza, or Ricordi & Co.'s American representatives, should call Puccini's attention to the fact that his employment of the National Anthem of the United States of America in "Madama Butterfly" is highly objectionable and might, in time, become offensive, although no offence was meant by him.

I "did" the first night of David Belasco's play "Madam Butterfly" for the New York *Herald*. The production occurred at the Herald Square Theatre, Broadway and Thirty-fifth Street, New York, March 5, 1900, with Blanche Bates as *Butterfly*. It was given with "Naughty Anthony," a farce-comedy also by Belasco, which had been a failure. The tragedy had been constructed with great rapidity from

43

The Complete Opera Book

John Luther Long's story, but its success was even swifter. At the Duke of York's Theatre, London, it was seen by Francis Nielsen, stage-manager of Covent Garden, who immediately sent word to Puccini urging him to come from Milan to London to see a play which, in his hands, might well become a successful opera. Puccini came at once, with the result that he created a work which has done its full share toward making the modern Italian lyric stage as flourishing as all unprejudiced critics concede it to be.

. The Milan production of "Madama Butterfly" was an utter failure. The audience hooted, the prima donna was in tears. The only person behind the scenes not disconcerted was the composer, whose faith in his work was so soon to be justified.

LA FANCIULLA DEL WEST

(THE GIRL OF THE GOLDEN WEST)

Opera in three acts by Puccini; words by C. Zangarini and G. Civini, after the play by David Belasco. Produced, Metropolitan Opera House, New York, December 10, 1910, with Destinn, Mattfeld, Caruso, Amato, Reiss, Didur, Dinh-Gilly, Pini Corsi, and De Segurola.

CHARACTERS

MINNIE		Soprano
JACK RANCE, sheriff		Baritone
DICK JOHNSON (Ramerrez.)		Tenor
NICK, bartender at the "Polka"		Tenor
ASHBY, Wells-Fargo agent		Bass
SONORA		Baritone
TRIN		Tenor
SID		Baritone
HANDSOME	Miners	Baritone
HARRY		Tenor
JOE		Tenor
HAPPY		Baritone
LARKENS		Bass
BILLY JACKRABBIT, an Indian redskin		Bass

DESTINN AS MINNIE, CARUSO AS JOHNSON, AND AMATO AS JACK RANCE
IN "THE GIRL OF THE GOLDEN WEST."

JOHN COATES IN "THE GIRL OF THE GOLDEN WEST."

Giacomo Puccini

WOWKLE, Billy's squaw..................... ......*Mezzo-Soprano*
JAKE WALLACE, a travelling camp minstrel..........*Baritone*
JOSÉ CASTRO, a greaser from Ramerrez's gang........*Bass*
A POSTILLON...................................*Tenor*
MEN OF THE CAMP

Time—1849–1850, the days of the gold fever.   *Place*—A
   mining-camp at the foot of the Cloudy Mountains, California.

Successful in producing "atmosphere" in "La Bohème,"
"Tosca," and "Madama Butterfly," Puccini has utterly
failed in his effort to do so in his "Girl of the Golden West."
Based upon an American play, the scene laid in America
and given in America for the first time on any stage, the
opera has not been, the more's the pity, a success.

In the first act, laid in the "Polka" bar-room, after a
scene of considerable length for the miners (intended, no
doubt, to create "atmosphere") there is an episode between
Rance and *Minnie*, in which it develops that *Rance* wants
to marry her, but that she does not care for him.   *Johnson*
comes in.   He and *Minnie* have met but once before, but
have been strongly attracted to each other.   She asks him
to visit her in her cabin, where they will be undisturbed by
the crowd, which has gone off to hunt for Ramerrez, head of
a band of outlaws, reported to be in the vicinity but which
soon may be back.

The scene of the second act is *Minnie's* cabin, which con-
sists of a room and loft.   After a brief scene for *Billy* and
Wowkle, *Minnie* comes in.   Through night and a blizzard
Johnson makes his way up the mountainside.   There is a
love scene—then noises outside.   People are approaching.
Not wishing to be found with *Johnson*, *Minnie* forces him
to hide.   *Rance* and others, who are on the trail of Ramerrez
and hope to catch or kill him any moment, come in to warn
her that *Johnson* is Ramerrez.   When they have gone, and
Johnson acknowledges that he is the outlaw, *Minnie*
denounces him and sends him out into the blizzard.   There

is a shot. *Johnson* sorely wounded staggers into the cabin. A knock at the door. *Rance's* voice. With *Minnie's* aid the wounded man reaches the loft where he collapses.

Rance enters, expecting to find *Johnson*. He is almost persuaded by *Minnie* that the fugitive is not there, when, through the loose timbers of the loft, a drop of blood falls on his hand. *Minnie* proposes that they play cards—*Johnson* to live, or she to marry the sheriff. They play. She cheats, and wins.

The third act is laid in the forest. *Johnson*, who has recovered and left *Minnie's* cabin, is caught, and is to be hung. But at the critical moment *Minnie* arrives, and her pleading moves the men to spare him, in spite of *Rance's* protests. They leave to begin a new life elsewhere.

In the score there is much recitative. It is not interesting in itself, nor is it made so by the insufficiently varied instrumental accompaniment. For the action of the play is too vigorous to find expression by means of the Debussyan manner that predominates in the orchestra. The most genuinely inspired musical number is *Johnson's* solo in the last act, when it seems certain that he is about to be executed.—"Ch'ella mi creda libero e lontano" (Let her believe that I have gained my freedom).

LA RONDINE

THE SWALLOW

The opera begins in Paris during the Second Empire. *Magda*, the heroine, is a *demi-mondaine* living under the protection of the rich banker *Rambaldo*. Satisfied with the luxuries he lavishes upon her, she longs for true affection, and is unable to stifle the remembrance of her first love, a poor young student. She meets *Ruggero*, who like her earlier love, is young and poor, and a student. At Bouilliers, the rendezvous of the gay life of Paris, *Ruggero* declares his love for *Magda*. They leave Paris for Nice, where they hope to lead an idyllic existence.

Ruggero looks forward to a life of perfect happiness. He writes to his parents asking their consent to his marriage with *Magda*. The reply is that if she is virtuous and honourable, she will be received with open arms. *Magda* now considers herself (like *Violetta* in "La Traviata") unworthy of *Ruggero's* love and lest she shall bring dishonour upon the man she loves, she parts with him. Other principal rôles are *Lisetta* and *Prunia*, and there are numerous second parts requiring first-rate artists.

In the second act of "La Rondine" is a quartet which, it is said, Puccini believes will rival that at the end of the third act in "La Bohème." "I have let my pen run," he is reported to have said, "and no other method suffices to obtain good results, in my opinion. No matter what marvellous technical effects may be worked up by lengthy meditation, I believe in heart in preference to head."

The opera was produced in March, 1917, in Monte Carlo, and during the summer of the same year, in Buenos Aires. Puccini intended to compose it with dialogue as a genuine opéra comique, but finally substituted recitative. The work is said to approach opéra comique in style. Reports regarding its success vary.

After the first Italian performance, San Carlo Theatre, Naples, February 26, 1918, Puccini, according to report, decided to revise "La Rondine." Revision, as in the case of "Madama Butterfly," may make a great success of it.

ONE-ACT OPERAS

Three one-act operas by Puccini have been composed for performance at one sitting. They are "Suor Angelica" (Sister Angelica), "Il Tabarro" (The Cloak), and "Gianni Schicchi." The motifs of these operas are sentiment, tragedy, and humour.

The scene of "Suor Angelica" is laid within the walls of a mountain convent, whither she has retired to expiate an unfortunate past. Her first contact with the outer world is through a visit from an aunt, who needs her signature to a document. Timidly she asks about the tiny mite, whom she was constrained to abandon before she entered the convent. Harshly the aunt replies that the child is dead. *Sister Angelica* decides to make an end to her life amid the flowers she loves. Dying, she appeals for pardon for her act of self-destruction. The doors of the convent church open, and a dazzling light pours forth revealing the Virgin Mary on the threshold surrounded by angels, who, intoning a sweet chorus, bear the poor, penitent, and weary soul to eternal peace. This little work is entirely for female voices.

The libretto of "Il Tabarro" is tragic. The great scene is between a husband and his wife. The husband has killed her lover, whose body he shows to his unfaithful wife, lifting from the ground the cloak (il tabarro) under which it is hidden.

The scene of "Il Tabarro" is laid on the deck of a Seine barge at sunset, when the day's work is over, and after dark. The husband is *Michele*, the wife *Giogetta*, the lover, *Luigi*, and there are two other bargemen. These latter go off after the day's work. *Luigi* lingers in the cabin. He persuades *Giogetta* that, when all is quiet on the barge, and it will be safe for him to return to her, she shall strike a match as a signal. He then goes.

Michele has suspected his wife. He reminds her of their early love, when he sheltered her under his cloak. *Giogetta*, however, receives these reminiscences coldly, feigns weariness, and retires to the cabin.

It has grown dark. *Michele* lights his pipe. *Luigi* thinking it is *Giogetta's* signal, clambers up the side of the barge, where he is seized and choked to death by *Michele*, who takes his cloak and covers the corpse with it.

Giacomo Puccini

Giogetta has heard sounds of a struggle. She comes on deck in alarm, but is somewhat reassured, when she sees *Michele* sitting alone and quietly smoking. Still somewhat nervous, however, she endeavours to atone for her frigidity toward him, but a short time before, by "making up" to him, telling him, among other things, that she well recalls their early love and wishes she could again find shelter in the folds of his big cloak. For reply, he raises the cloak, and lets her see *Luigi's* corpse.

I have read another synopsis of this plot, in which *Michele* forces his wife's face close to that of her dead lover. At the same moment, one of the other bargemen, whose wife also had betrayed him, returns brandishing the bloody knife, with which he has slain her. The simpler version surely is more dramatic than the one of cumulative horrors.

When the action of "Gianni Schicchi" opens one *Donati* has been dead for two hours. His relations are thinking of the will. A young man of the house hands it to his mother but exacts the promise that he shall marry the daughter of neighbour *Schicchi*. When the will is read, it is found that *Donati* has left his all to charity. *Schicchi* is called in, and consulted. He plans a ruse. So far only those in the room know of *Donati's* demise. The corpse is hidden. *Schicchi* gets into bed, and, when the *Doctor* calls, imitates the dead man's voice and pretends he wants to sleep. The lawyer is sent for. *Schicchi* dictates a new will—in favour of himself, and becomes the heir, in spite of the anger of the others.

www.ingramcontent.com/pod-product-compliance
Lightning Source LLC
Chambersburg PA
CBHW021205090426
42740CB00008B/1238